United States Congress Senate, Rufus B. Bullock

Remarks of Gov. Bullock to the Judiciary Committee of the Senate

In Reconstruction of Georgia. March 2, 1870

United States Congress Senate, Rufus B. Bullock

Remarks of Gov. Bullock to the Judiciary Committee of the Senate
In Reconstruction of Georgia. March 2, 1870

ISBN/EAN: 9783337161484

Printed in Europe, USA, Canada, Australia, Japan

Cover: Foto ©Suzi / pixelio.de

More available books at **www.hansebooks.com**

REMARKS

OF

GOV. BULLOCK

TO THE

JUDICIARY COMMITTEE

OF THE SENATE,

In Re.

RECONSTRUCTION OF GEORGIA.

MARCH 2, 1870.

———

WASHINGTON:
CHRONICLE PRINT, 511 NINTH STREET.
1870.

The Honorable Chairman and members of the Judiciary Committee of the Senate:

I have been placed in possession of a printed pamphlet containing a revised edition of the papers read before your honorable committee, on the 9th of February last, by Messrs J. H. Caldwell and J. E. Bryant, together with an appendix containing a paper signed " N. L. Angier, Treasurer of Georgia," and entitled " Governor Bullock's financial operations," and also nine pages of printed matter under the following title :

"Before the Judiciary Committee on Saturday, February 12, 1870, Judge Gibson, on behalf of Governor Bullock, read an argument, to which Mr. Caldwell replied in substance as follows :"

This reply of Mr. Caldwell, together with the paper signed by Angier, I desire to notice before your honorable committee shall have formed final conclusions and agreed upon a report in what is commonly known as the " Georgia Question."

As the exact subject matter before the committee, by action of the Senate, does not appear in any of the printed papers which I have been able to obtain possession of, I must admit that I have no very well defined information as to what branch of the " Georgia Question" is formally before your honorable committee.

My first information that the affairs of Georgia were to be considered by your honorable committee was derived from the note of your honorable Chairman, dated the 6th day of February, informing me that Mr. J. H. Caldwell, C. K. Osgood, and others had applied to lay before your honorable committee *certain facts* in regard to the organization of the Legislature and the state of affairs in Georgia, and at the same time extending to me an invitation to be present on the following Wednesday, at 11 o'clock.

At that time Mr. Caldwell and Mr. Bryant appeared as speakers, and to the "certain facts" (many of which, by the way, proved to be very uncertain) in regard to the organization of the Legislature and the state of affairs in Georgia, reply was made by me and presented to your honorable committee in print, under date of the 10th of February, and will be found on pages 27 to 57, inclusive, of the pamphlet entitled "Georgia before the Senate Judiciary Committee, February 9th, 1870," and to which the attention of your honorable committee is respectfully invited.

The statement, therefore, that "Judge Gibson appeared in behalf of Governor Bullock," is not correct. Judges Gibson, Harrell, and Parrott, together with Mr. Conley, the President of the Senate, and Mr. Tweedy, of the House, united in a communication to your honorable committee, printed in a pamphlet entitled "The Admission of Georgia."

These gentlemen are all men of high character and standing, and speak for themselves. While I agree with what they say in their communication, they do not represent *me*, more than they do every other *Republican* in Georgia. It is not probable, however, that either of the gentlemen would have presented their views to your

honorable committee had it not been for the unwar-
rantable and insolent assault made upon the character of
Judge Gibson by Mr. Bryant in his remarks on the 9th
instant.

In my former communications to your honorable committee, I endeavored to avoid, as far as possible, any
remarks of a party or partisan character. It was my
purpose to avoid speaking of either the Republican or
the Democratic parties in this matter. But I hope that your
honorable committee will overlook the impropriety of my
doing so at this time, for it seems to be called for by the
character of the communication to which I desire to
reply.

Mr. Caldwell assumes that under the former organization there was a Republican majority in the Lower
House. He says:

"There were several strict party votes among them that
which elected the Speaker, from which it appeared that
there was a Republican majority of one in the House,"
etc. "Since then, the Republican majority has been
increased by the deaths which have occurred."

The fact, however, is that a Republican was elected
Speaker by the following vote: Hon. R. L. McWhorter,
76 votes; W. P. Price, dem., 74 votes; W. F. Holden,
rep., [voted for by Mr. McWhorter,] one vote, making
77 Republican votes to 74 Democratic votes, as will be
found recorded in the Journal of that House on page 12,
under the old organization. This election took place on
Saturday, and on the following Monday, at nine and
a-half o'clock, a number of additional members having
arrived and been sworn in, the House proceeded to the
election of a clerk, at which time, M. A. Hardin, Dem-

ocrat, received 83 votes, Mr. S. C. Johnson, Republican, received 78 votes.

Thus the Republican vote had been increased by two, and the Democratic vote by thirteen. From that day until the present organization, there never was a Republican majority in the House of Representatives.

It was this same Legislature which Mr. Caldwell claims to have been republican, that, by a vote of 95 yeas to 43 nays, adopted a report which declared that John Long, of the County of Carroll, was eligible—a man who, as was shown by the report, prior to the late war held the offices of Justice of the Inferior Court and Clerk of the Superior Court, and during the rebellion held the office of County Treasurer. This is only a sample case ; many others equally, ineligible were by that House declared to be eligible.

Mr. Caldwell asserts that " had each member been left to his own conscience in the late organization, to qualify or not, just as the law allowed him to do, etc., * * it is likely that a sufficient number would have refused to qualify to make a republican majority in the two houses of 15 or 20."

With the exception of the three men who were declared to be ineligible by order of the General commanding the District, each member *was* "left to his own conscience," etc., and had there been a rigid enforcement of a literal construction of the disqualifications fixed by the Act of December 22, or by the previous acts, which declared that no person disqualified by the third section of the Fourteenth Amendment shall hold office in either of the States named in that act, Georgia being one of them, there would have been at least thirteen other members excluded from the present organization who were permitted to participate in it.

These thirteen persons took the oath prescribed in the Act of December 22, notwithstanding the fact that they were candidates for, and were elected to, offices under the State Government at an election held on the first Tuesday of January, 1861, and were commissioned in the offices to which they were elected on or about the 25th day of the same month, and continued from that time forward, for various periods, to perform the duties of their offices during the rebellion. These persons claim that by the the fact that the ordinance of secession was adopted by the Secession Convention of Georgia on the 19th day of the same month, a date which occurred a few days after their election and a few days before they were commissioned, they were shielded from the effect of the disqualifying clauses of the Act of Dec. 22d.

The claim thus set up was regarded favorably by the Commander of the District, in deference to the opinion of the Honorable Attorney General of the United States, and these thirteen members were permitted to retain their seats in the Legislature.

It will be observed, therefore, that the greatest liberality has been exercised in construing the act of December 22, so as not to affect unfavorably any person who might, by any possibility, be deemed eligible.

Mr. Caldwell attempts to cast a reflection or doubt upon the republicanism of the Speaker of the House of Representatives by saying:

"It was Speaker McWhorter's rulings which led to the expulsion of the colored members," &c.

The rulings to which Mr. Caldwell refers were—

"That no member, whose eligibility had been questioned by the committee, and which question was involved in the report, was entitled to vote therein."

And on page 40 of the Journal of the House of Representatives of the old organization, we find that when the question of the eligibility of certain white members was under consideration, Mr. Bryant, of Richmond County, raised the point of order that—

"No member whose eligibility had been questioned by the committee, and which question was involved in the report, was entitled to vote thereon."

The Speaker made this ruling, and decided that they were not entitled to vote. Mr. Crawford, (Dem.) of Barton County, appealed from the decision of the Speaker, upon which appeal the yeas and nays were required to be recorded, and resulted in yeas 84, nays 74. Among those who voted to sustain the Speaker in this ruling *we find the name of Mr. Caldwell.*

When the report of the committee upon privileges and elections, declaring colored men not eligible to hold offices or seats in the Legislature, was made, we find upon page 224 of the Journal of the House, old organization, that Mr. Scott, Democrat, of Floyd, made the point of order—

"That upon the decision of the question now under consideration, the persons whose seats are contested and herein involved are not allowed to vote. Mr. Price, the Speaker *pro tem.*, being in the chair, decided the point well taken. Mr. Bryant appealed from the decision of the chair, upon which appeal the yeas and nays were required, and resulted in yeas 90, nays 19."

Among those who voted in the affirmative—voted to sustain the ruling, not of the Speaker proper. Mr. McWhorter, but of the Speaker pro tempore. Mr. Price, a Democrat then in the chair, will be found *the name of Mr. Caldwell!!!* Upon the final vote, by which the colored men were excluded, Mr. Caldwell was *absent*: but a few days after the expulsion had been accomplished, he sought and obtained permission to have his vote recorded in the negative. It is painful to thus destroy Mr. Caldwell's consistency by referring to his political record, but the truth of history demands it."

The general sentiment of the community at that time —the great Democratic convention at New York having by its resolutions declared the reconstruction acts to be revolutionary, unconstitutional, and void, and intimated that the governments established under those acts should be dissipated—the threatening letters received by republican members from their respective homes, together with the well-known impossibility of preventing, by their votes, they being largely in the minority, the expulsion of the colored members, will account for the small Republican vote which is found in opposition to the revolutionary action of the rebel majority in the organization.

From the foregoing I think your honorable committee will agree with me that the statements of Mr. Caldwell that the Lower House of the Legislature was a Republican body after the admission to it of all the men declared by General Meade's order to have been elected, irrespective of their eligibility under the law, is effectually disposed of, and that some light has been thrown upon the consistency of the honorable gentleman's political record.

Mr. Caldwell further proceeds to refer to a very important branch of this question by saying :

B

" Your attention has been directed to the leading idea
of the Governor's report, viz : that the purpose of the late
act of Congress was to set aside the first organization of
the Legislature as illegal, and render all its acts void,
and especially the validity of election of United States
Senators and State officers. This construction of the
meaning of the act grounds itself upon the idea that the
number of ineligible persons supposed to be in the body
vitiated the whole body and all its acts."

This allegation is not supported by anything presented
by Mr. Caldwell, nor is it supported by any fact whatever.
The purpose of the late act of Congress I conceive to
have been just exactly what is announced in its title.
namely, *to promote the reconstruction of the State of
Georgia.*

After thus giving a false statement of my construction
of the act, he adds :

" This construction of the meaning of the act grounds
itself upon the idea that the number of ineligible persons
supposed to be in the body vitiated the whole body and
all its acts ;"

And then proceeds to argue that, if any number less
than a majority were disqualified members, the body—a
qualified majority being a quorum—were competent to
act, &c. The argument of Mr. Caldwell on this point
is a very weak imitation of the very able and comprehensive minority report made by your Honorable Chairman on the same subject, January 25th, 1869.

On the 25th of January, 1869, your honorable committee made a report to the Senate, [40th Congress, 3d
session, report of committee 192, on the credentials of
Joshua Hill, claiming to be a Senator elect from Georgia.]

In that report your honorable committee arrived at the
conclusion that the right of Mr. Hill, if regularly elected,

to a seat in the Senate depended upon three important considerations:

"First. Did the Legislature of Georgia, regularly organized in accordance with the Constitution of the United States, the laws of Congress, and the Constitution of Georgia, duly ratify the fourteenth amendment, and comply with the various conditions imposed by the act of June 25, 1868.

Second. Had the Legislature and people of Georgia, subsequent to such compliance with said act of Congress, committed such acts of usurpation and outrage as to place the State in a condition unfit to be represented in Congress?

Third. Whether on the whole case, taking the action of Georgia, both before and since the pretended ratification of the fourteenth amendment, a civil government has been established in that State which Congress ought to recognize."

After reciting the result of a thorough and careful investigation, your honorable committee concludes as follows:

"Wherefore your committee feel called upon to recommend that Mr. Hill be not allowed to take a seat in the Senate for the reason that Georgia *is not entitled to representation in Congress*."

In another part of the same report your honorable committee disposes of the point now revived by Mr. Caldwell by saying:

" For the purposes of this report, however, your committee did not deem it necessary to ascertain the number of disqualified persons admitted, but the fact that *any* were knowingly admitted was not only a violation of the fourteenth amendment and *a failure to comply with the requirements of Congress*, but manifests a disposition to

disobey and defy the authority of the United States. If
one can be admitted, why not all? And will it be contended that if the entire body had been composed of men
who had usurped the functions of the Legislature against
the express provisions of the reconstruction acts, they
could have complied with the provisions of those acts so
as to create any obligation on the part of Congress to
receive their Senators and Representatives? Your committee are of opinion that the act of June 25, 1868, which
required that the constitutional amendment should be
duly ratified must be held to mean that it must be ratified
by a Legislature which has in good faith substantially
complied with all the requirements of law providing for
its organization."

Mr. Hill was, therefore, refused his seat, notwithstanding the very able and comprehensive minority
report, made at the same time by your honorable Chairman, to the effect that, even admitting a number of members to have been disqualified, there was not a sufficient
number of that character to render invalid the proceedings of the body, and that, if the Legislature was properly organized when it elected Mr. Hill, the fact that it
subsequently became disorganized ought not to effect
his election. The opinion of the majority of your honorable committee, however, seems to have been sus-
tained by the action of both Houses of Congress, and by
the President in the passage and approval of the act of
December 22, to promote the reconstruction of the State
of Georgia. That act provides for the reassembling of
the persons declared to have been elected by General
Meade, to wit: the same persons who assembled and
made the organization which was inquired into by your
honorable committee in January, 1869, and that the reorganization shall be effected by the exclusion from its mem-
bership of all persons who held office under the United

States or a State Government and thereafter participated
in the rebellion, or held office under a government
organized in rebellion, &c. It provided, also, that the
persons who were qualified under this act should proceed
to *reorganize the Legislature by the election of its officers.*
Does not this determine in the most positive manner that
in the opinion of Congress, and of the President, the old
organization was not only not competent to " *duly* ratify
the Fourteenth Amendment," but was not competent to
elect its own officers? and that neither Congress or the
President was bound to recognize its political acts as
entitling the State to representation? And it is a very
natural conclusion that if the old organization was not
considered by Congress to have duly ratified the Fourteenth Amendment in such a way as to bind Congress to
recognize such ratification, and had not elected its own
officers, *it could not have duly elected United States
Senators.*

There is no half-way ground in this matter. Either
the government of Georgia is " Provisional" to-day, or
the action of Congress in passing the act of December 22,
1869, and the President's assignment of General Terry
to duty as District Commander under the reconstruction
laws, cannot be defended. The act of December 22,
1869, by assuming that the Legislature had never been
legally organized *ipso facto*, placed the State under the
reconstruction laws. Such is the inevitable logic of the
requirement that there shall be a *new* organization, and
such *must* be the interpretation to justify the President's
orders to General Terry, and to render lawful General
Terry's acts under those orders in interfering to preserve
life and property, arresting and confining assassins,
house-burners, negro-whippers, &c., and in removing
sheriffs who refused to do their duty, and in appointing

others in their stead. If the Legislature was ever lawfully organized, though Congress might undertake to purge it, or to reseat persons it had improperly expelled, it would not undertake to order its reorganization.

There is but one way out of the inextricable confusion and illegality into which this effort to sustain the election of Senators by the old organization will lead, and that is to give the act of Dec. 22d, 1869. the full scope and meaning that was given to it by the President in his order assigning General Terry to the command of the " district" of Georgia—to wit : as a declaration that Georgia was still subject to the reconstruction laws ; still without any " legal State government" competent to take part in, or to be recognized by, the Government of the United States as a State government *de jure*.

Nor does the fact that the Executive Department and the House of Representatives have each indirectly recognized the government of Georgia as a " Legal State Government." and therefore entitled to be represented in Congress, at all militate against this view.

The point on which the Congressional scheme of reconstruction turns seems to be this. Ex-President Johnson contended that when the Executive had recognized a State Government as a legal State Government, there was nothing to be done to complete the process of reconstruction but for each House, under its power " to judge of the election and qualification of its members " to proceed independently, and decide upon the admission of the members of the several Houses. And in an elaborate message he communicated these views to Congress.

That body forthwith by a joint resolution repudiated this doctrine, and declared that none of the late Rebel

States should be entitled to representation until Congress so declared by law.

If the House of Representatives of the 40th Congress, under a mistaken belief, caused by false representations that the Legislature had in good faith purged itself of ineligible members, admitted to their seats the Georgia Representatives without any declaration " by law" having been made that the State *was* entitled to representation, it was a simple act of one House, and not in accord with the joint resolution in which the fundamental doctrine of reconstruction was declared. Each House is the judge of the election and qualification of its own members, but neither House of Congress can by itself conclusively decide when one of the late rebel States is entitled to be represented in Congress.

So soon as the facts of the Georgia matter were made known and understood—so soon as it was made apparent that the Legislature of Georgia had not been legally organized—Congress, both Houses concurring, adopted the act of 22d December, 1869, requiring the Legislature to be reorganized. And this was done with great unanimity, notwithstanding the previous action of the House of Representatives, which action by the House, as we have said, was induced by the political fraud perpetrated by men whose character and intentions were not suspected, until their expulsion of the negroes had directed inquiry into the manner of the organization of the Legislature, to ascertain how it was possible for such action to occur, if men who were disqualified under the reconstruction laws had been excluded. Then it was that the facts were ascertained which led to the report of your honorable committee in January, and the action of Congress and the President. in December, 1869.

It is therefore clear that under the act of December 22, 1869, and under the orders of the President by virtue of that act, and under the proceedings of General Terry under those orders, that Georgia was not entitled to representation in Congress, and the Legislature of 1868 was no more competent to elect Senators, and organize a State government *de jure* than was the Legislature of 1865–66.   In those years, under the supervision of President Johnson, Mr. Jenkins was inaugurated as Governor of the State.   The Legislature was organized and had two protracted sessions, and the military jurisdiction of the United States was withdrawn.   Two Senators were elected ; the Thirteenth Amendment to the Constitution was ratified, and from January, 1865, to March, 1867, for all local purposes, and for such national purposes as the President could control, a State government was in operation.   Yet Congress, by the act of March 2, 1867, declared that there was no legal State government in existence in the State, repudiated the election of Senators, and under its power to guarantee each State a republican government, adopted the Congressional scheme of reconstruction.

In close analogy to this, Congress, the law-making power, treating as inconclusive the action of General Meade, as well as the action of the House of Representatives of the Fortieth Congress, passed the act of December 22, 1869, and this was supplemented by the necessary action of the President.

The local legislation of the body in 1865–1866, has always been recognized as valid until repealed, as well as the ordinary legislation of the body assembled in 1868–1869.   This point, however is treated in full in the appendix to which reference is made.

Such is the inevitable logic of what has been done,

and this inevitable logic must be answered, before a Legislature which, by act of Congress, has been declared incompetent to elect its own officers can be held competent to have ratified amendments to the Constitution and elected Senators to the Congress of the United States.

It does not follow, however, that the ordinary local legislation of that body is not valid as acts *de facto* until repealed by a legally organized body. In order to defeat, if possible, the full effect of the action of Congress in upsetting rebel machinations, the suggestion has been rigorously made that State bonds were to be repudiated, contracts violated, laws ignored, etc. But this is mere bosh. The only State bonds of Georgia which have been sold since the war, were issued under the authority of the Legislature of 1865. Upon this point I invite your attention to my communication to the Legislature of February 16 last, herewith transmitted in the Appendix ''A.''

Objection has heretofore been made by gentlemen who sought the attention of your Honorable Committee, to the fact that persons who were qualified were awarded the seats claimed by men who were disqualified. This action was taken by the body itself after it had reorganized, by the election of its presiding officer, and by a vote which would not have been changed had the three persons who were by General Terry decided to be disqualified, been permitted to participate in the proceedings. Hence if the organization had been lawfully perfected by the election of its presiding officer, the admission of these persons was the act of that lawful body. My own opinion is that it was in the power of the General commanding the District of Georgia under the reconstruction acts to have enforced such action. Your attention is invited to my views upon this point, as embodied in my correspondence

c

with the Major General commanding the District of Georgia, a copy of which is printed in the appendix marked "B."

I also invite your attention to the views and conclusions of General Terry upon this subject, printed in appendix marked "C." My impression and understanding is that the majority of the House based their action in this matter upon the same ground taken by General Terry, and for the reasons therein set forth.

We should keep in view the fact that at the election, when these persons who are disqualified were candidates, the publicly-proclaimed object of the party with which they acted was to defeat the reconstruction policy by voting down the new constitution. To do this the more effectually by bringing out their voters, the Democratic party nominated candidates for every office provided for in the new constitution. Of course, if their primal object—the defeat of the new constitution—was accomplished, there would be no offices for their candidates to fill; hence they were selected for their popularity on their war record, without regard to their eligibility under the law, although all parties had been put on notice by a general order from General Mead of what the law fixed as disqualification.

My opponent was the gallant Lieutenant General Gordon, who won his fame in the Confederate ranks at Gettysburg; and so throughout the State candidates were nominated not because they were qualified to hold office under the law; not because their party expected or desired them to hold office under the reconstruction constitution, but simply and solely to bring out votes by their rebel record against the constitution. And I respectfully submit that the strict application of the law and the parliamentary rule in these cases becomes marked *retribu-tive justice.*

Mr. Caldwell, however, in his last paper before your honorable committee, says :

"We care but little for the irregularities of the present organization, and are willing for it to stand if Governor Bullock may not be allowed to carry out his ruinous designs. If you shall suffer everything that preceded the act to promote reconstruction to be ripped up and the official terms to be extended as the Governor proposes, it will throw us into inextricable confusion, and perhaps involve us in financial ruin. If you recognize the valid-ity of the Legislature prior to the expulsion of the colored members, let all the acts of the body up to that time stand, admit the present Senators elect, and confine the official terms within the limits prescribed by the ordi-nance of the convention and the constitution, we are con-tent," etc., etc.

It has never been proposed to extend any officer's official term, although there are plenty of men in office in Georgia to-day, who have *"extended their term"* since the time when Jeff Davis was elected President of C. S. A.

All that I have said upon that subject is that when the organization of the Legislature shall have been accepted by Congress, and the State shall have been admitted to representation and thereby become a State in the Union, that then the members of the Legislature will enter as members *dejure* upon the constitutional term for which they were elected.

The convention which framed the constitution, adopted an ordinance to provide for the election of civil officers at the same time of voting for or against the constitu-tion, which, in its preamble, says :

" *Whereas*, All civil offices of the State are only provisional until this State is represented in Congress; and *whereas*, the interests of Georgia require that all civil offices should be filled by loyal citizens, according to the provisions of the constitution being framed by this Convention at the earliest practicable moment and for the purpose of avoiding any unnecessary delay or loss of time and useless expense to the State," etc.

It was thus clearly provided that the persons elected at the time of the ratification of the constitution should simply be *provisional officers* until the State was admitted. When that event took place, they then became the officers of the State government in fact—the constitution which had been ratified by the people became of force by the recognition of the State by Congress, and the regular terms of office would then be decided and restricted by that constitution.

Certainly no loyal man—no man who has the welfare and safety of the government established under the new constitution in Georgia at heart can ask or wish to deprive his friends of the opportunity of carrying out, in good faith and effectively, the provisions of that constitution, the securing of equal justice and equal rights before the law for all of our citizens, the opportunity to vote undisturbed by the intimidations of Ku Klux assassins, and the establishment of free schools, as provided in that instrument.

It is quite reasonable that Mr. Caldwell should say, speaking for himself and the party opposing the reconstruction policy, whom he now represents:

"We care but little for the irregularities of the present organization. If you recognize the validity of the Legislature prior to the expulsion of the colored members, admit the Senators elect," etc., etc.

For little *do* they care for anything, either regular or irregular, if the seating of Messrs. Hill and Miller can only be accomplished, and their friends be permitted to go through the farce of an election similar to the reign of anarchy and terror which is politely termed, *"carrying the State for Seymour and Blair."*

What loyal men ask and expect at the hands of Congress is that the high position which Congress has taken in putting down the usurpations of the Georgia rebels shall be maintained, and that now when an organization has been perfected in accordance with the late act to promote the reconstruction of Georgia, whereby the Legislative power rests in the hands of the friends of the new system of government, they shall be permitted to carry out the measures which the people adopted in voting for the Constitution; and thus, by their own legislation, provide means for their protection, so that when the regular legal time for the election shall have arrived, it may be a free and fair expression of political preference on the part of the voter, whether he be poor, ignorant and black, or rich, arrogant and white. Whether he be Republican or Democrat, Radical or Ku-Klux.

It seems to serve the purpose of these people who are endeavoring to prevent the state of facts to which I have just referred, to allege that I have " designs " which are " ruinous " to the State, and that all sorts of fearful calamities will inevitably befall the State if a Republican Legislature is not checked and dispersed with as little delay as possible. But where can be found a safe foundation whereon to rest a belief that a legislature composed of men, a majority of whom have risked their lives and their property in their efforts to carry out the Congressional policy of reconstruction and establish a state government founded upon the consent of *all* the governed without regard to race or color, will fail to carefully guard and protect their own interests and the interests of the people they represent by promptly bringing up for investigation and, if found guilty, to punishment, any officer of that government who fails or neglects to perform his duty, or wilfully violates the laws by which he is to be controlled? Are the friends of the new constitution less likely to guard it and punish violations under it, than its opponents and its enemies?

The Republicans endured the government established by President Johnson in Georgia for nearly two years beyond the term for which that government was elected, and made little, if any complaints; and now why should the Democrats of Georgia, through their mouth-pieces here, make such a terrible outcry against a Legislature with a Republican majority which does not propose to extend its term, but simply to hold the term for which it was elected? Why should these Democrats plead that the time occupied with their revolutionary proceedings, during which the government of the State was provisional, should be now counted against the term of the lawfully organized body?

The answer is found in their fear of losing their power and control, and their opportunity to longer obstruct the establishment of a loyal Republican government in Georgia.

So far as I am personally concerned, it is well-known to my personal friends and to my business acquaintances that I retain the office I now hold at great pecuniary sacrifice to myself, and there is certainly little comfort in being the target of either Billingsgate or bullets. But as I have heretofore assured the President and General Terry, I now assure you that my resignation is at their service. My only ambition is to firmly establish a Republican government in Georgia, and if that can be promoted in the least degree by my retirement, it will be a pleasure for me to yield the office. Rebel faultfinding and abuse, however, will never accomplish that result.

I am unwilling to believe, and the men who have risked their lives, their property, and their good name in sustaining the great principles of republican liberty in Georgia, are unwilling to believe that this honorable committee will listen to or be controlled by the pleas presented here by the enemies of good government and the enemies of our domestic peace, even though they be presented, as they now are, by representatives who have heretofore acted with your friends, and therefore, now hope the more effectually to forward the purposes of their new found allies.

We believe that your action will be in harmony with these great principles, and of a character to sustain the party which has upheld them. With such action, the friends of good order and good government in Georgia will soon disclose their ability to maintain themselves.

If, however, such action should be taken as will stimulate and encourage a renewal of the active hostility to the Government and its friends which has now, since the late action of Congress, in a great measure subsided, we shall hope that, upon a more thorough investigation and full consideration of the great issues involved, the American Congress, which has never yet failed gallantly and consistently to uphold the right in the great struggle which is now nearly closing, and to uphold that right, too, even when the most insidious attempts, under guises the most deceitful, have been made against it, will render its verdict in favor of loyalty and justice, and against treason and treachery.

Until that verdict is rendered we shall labor for the right, and with that verdict we shall be content.

RUFUS B. BULLOCK.

There are some references of a personal character that I take the liberty of presenting to your honorable committee in an appendix, and to which your leisurely attention is respectfully invited.

APPENDIX A.

—

MESSAGE.

ATLANTA, GA., February 16, 1870.

To the Senate and House of Representatives

of the Provisional Legislature:

Some misapprehension having arisen as to the effect of the Act of Congress of December 22, 1869, upon the ordinary legislative acts of the Legislatures of 1868–'69. I deem it proper to say that, in my judgment, the Act of Congress referred to does not render invalid any of the ordinary laws passed by those bodies.

The Reconstruction Acts of March 3, 1867, and July 19, 1867, in express terms declared that "no legal State governments" existed in the States therein named; yet the Ordinances of the Convention of 1865, and the Acts of the Legislatures of 1865 and 1866, have been uniformly, by the military authorities and by our own Courts, held legal and binding. The "Sealing ordinance" of the Convention of 1865, "the Evidence law" of 1866, both Acts of immense importance, were, during the whole administrations of General Pope and General Meade, enforced by the Courts as valid and binding laws; yet these Acts were passed by bodies which Congress declared to be Legislatures of no "legal State governments."

General Pope and General Meade were put in command in this State to enforce "the laws." The Courts of Georgia sitting under the administration of the military authorities of the United States, never for a moment seem to have thought that the Acts of the Legislatures of 1865 and 1866 were not laws, and yet Congress had in express terms declared that "no legal State government existed in the State."

It would seem from this action that the declaration of Congress "that no legal State governments exist in the late rebel States," must be understood in a qualified sense, to wit: no legal State, competent to take part in the Government of the Union, and proper to be recognized as State governments under the Constitution of the United States.

It was not the intent of Congress, by any of its reconstruction legislation, to render invalid any of the laws passed by the Legislatures it subsequently declared illegal, except so far as those laws were obnoxious to the Constitution and laws of the United States.

It is true, it has not been the policy to permit legislative assemblies, as such, to convene and legislate, except for specific purposes during the military regime; but the whole practice of the Govern-

D

ment has been to recognize as valid, laws actually passed and not repudiated by the United States.

The simple fact that from March, 1867, to July, 1868, the Courts of this State, during the administrations of Generals Pope and Meade, and before the Convention of 1868 had ratified those laws, administered without question the Ordinances of the Convention of 1865, and the acts of the Legislatures of 1865 and 1866, is a judicial determination of the highest tribunals known to our law, that the ordinary laws of said bodies were valid and binding as the acts of a Legislature *de facto*, however illegal the bodies might themselves have been as "State Legislatures," in view of the reconstruction acts.

During the existence of the military supervision, meeting of legislative bodies, except for specific purposes, have been deemed incompatible with the actual state of affairs : but in all the States, laws passed by bodies meeting as such, when the military power was in fact withdrawn, have been uniformly recognized and acted upon as valid and binding.

It is, therefore, I think, apparent, from the uniform action of the courts, and of the United States authorities, that the laws of the Legislature of 1868 and 1869, and its acts which were not of a political character, are perfectly valid, notwithstanding the United States, by the act of December 22, 1869, has, in effect, declared that "no legal State Government existed in this State" at that time. And that the impression which is sought to be created that contracts are invalidated, that State bonds are repudiated, and that corporations, organized upon the basis of the late legislation, are without legal foundation, is entirely groundless. Such impression is only created for the purpose of misleading the public mind, and defeating the full effect and true intent and purpose of the Reconstruction Acts. Argument upon this point seems to be superfluous, added to the material fact that our bonds are saleable at a higher rate than those of any other Southern State: and that the bonds of railroads which have been endorsed under the authority of the legislation of 1868, are selling at their full value.

It has been suggested to me from various quarters, that it would be wise for your body to take some action for the temporary relief of the people from the present pressure for the payment of the war debts contracted before 1865; now made doubly burdensome by the late decision of the Supreme Court of the United States, that those contracted before 1862 are payable in gold.

As, however, in my judgment, until your action to complete the reconstruction of the State is accepted by Congress, it is not proper for you to undertake general legislation, I would respectfully suggest that you adopt some resolution expressive of the wishes of the General Assembly on this subject, with the hope that the General commanding may, by his order, cause the same to be enforced.

When the last step in the reconstruction work shall have been taken by the declaration of the result of the Senatorial election, I would respectfully recommend that a recess be taken for such a time as may to you seem best, pending the action of Congress for our admission.

RUFUS B. BULLOCK,
Provisional Governor.

APPENDIX B.

ATLANTA, GA., January 19, 1870.

GENERAL: Inclosed I hand you the application of William Guilford, colored, to be awarded the seat of J. C. Drake, a disqualified man, who received the highest number of votes in Upson county. Had the election been held under civil State authority, and were the legislative organization subject to civil jurisdiction, I should most certainly issue the certificate to Guilford.

This is a sample case, similar to a number of others, and if decided in the affirmative will insure justice to the colored race through a loyal Legislature.

I respectfully invite your attention to the inclosed argument in favor of such a course.

I am, general, very respectfully, your obedient servant,
RUFUS B. BULLOCK,
Provisional Governor.

MAJOR GENERAL TERRY,
Commanding District of Georgia.

ATLANTA, *January* 17, 1870.

GEORGIA, *Fulton County:*

The petition of William Guilford, (colored,) of the county of Upson and State aforesaid, respectfully showeth unto your Excellency that, under and by virtue of General Orders Nos. 39 and 40, issued by General Meade, dated, respectively, Atlanta, Georgia, March 14 and 15, 1868, an election was held in the county of Upson, beginning on the 20th day of April, 1868, and continuing four days, for Governor, members of Congress, members of the General Assembly, and other officers of this State; that, at said election, J. C. Drake and your petitioner were candidates, in said county of Upson, for a seat in the House of Representatives of this State; that at the time when the said election was held the said Drake was disqualified from holding office under the acts of Congress, (see act to admit the State of North Carolina, * * Georgia, * * June 25, 1868,) and that your petitioner was qualified; that, on the 25th day of June, Major General Meade issued General Orders No. 90, Headquarters Third Military District, announcing "that from the returns made by the boards of registration of the election held as aforesaid * * it appears that * * J. C. Drake, of Upson county, * * was elected Representative in the General Assembly;" that the said General Meade failed and the General Assembly refused to hear the application of your petitioner, showing that the said Drake being disqualified, your petitioner was, under the laws then and now of force, the legally elected Representative, and should have been awarded the seat.

Your petitioner further showeth unto your excellency that, under the recent act of Congress dated December 22, 1869, entitled "An act to promote the reconstruction of the State of Georgia," the second section of the said act requires one of the two oaths to be taken by the person claiming a seat in either branch of the general assembly. Said section concludes as follows : "And every person claiming to be so elected, who shall refuse or decline, or neglect, or be unable to take one of said oaths or affirmations above provided, shall not be admitted to a seat in said senate or house of representatives, or to a participation in the proceedings thereof, but shall be ineligible to such seat."

Your petitioner further showeth that said Drake has refused, declined, and neglected to take the oath required by act of Congress above mentioned, hence is ineligible to a seat in the house of representatives in this State.

Your petitioner further showeth that, under an ordinance of the late constitutional convention of this State, as appears on page 387 of the journal of said convention, as well as by the provisions of the present constitution of this State, and said recent act of Congress, he is qualified to hold a seat in said house of representatives.

Your petitioner further showeth that, under the fourteenth article of the Constitution of the United States, said Drake cannot hold a seat in the general assembly of this State, which has been demonstrated by his refusal to qualify as required by recent act of Congress; which enforces said fourteenth article.

Your petitioner further showeth that, under the law of this State, as appears in section 121, Irwin's code, it is provided that, if at any popular election to fill any office, the person elected is constitutionally ineligible, the person having the next highest number of votes, who is eligible, whenever a plurality elects, shall be declared elected and be qualified and commissioned to such office.

Your petitioner further showeth that he did, at said election in said county of Upson, receive the next highest number of votes to said Drake ; and under and by virtue of the law above cited, is entitled to a seat in the house of representatives of this State, after having filed with the secretary of State the oath required by said recent act of Congress, and respectfully asks your excellency to allow him to qualify and take his seat as a member of the house of representatives of this State.

Respectfully,

WILLIAM GUILFORD.

His excellency RUFUS B. BULLOCK,
Provisional Governor of the State of Georgia.

In the enforcement of the act of December 22, 1869, two questions have presented themselves:

1st. Who is the final judge of eligibility of a member of the legislature; the member himself, the house to which he claims to be elected, or the general commanding?

2d. If any are found ineligible, is it proper that the commanding general direct the next highest person voted for to take his place, and participate in the reorganization, or if this is to be left to the houses after they are organized?

On these questions the following observations are submitted:

When at the cessation of armed resistance by the rebels, in May, 1865, the several States lately in rebellion were found, under the Constitution of the United States, to be absolutely without legal civil government, undoubtedly it devolved upon the United States, in the then status in fact of affairs, and under article 4, section 4, of the federal Constitution, to see to it that legal civil government should be re-established.

It would seem to follow as a necessary incident to this power that the United States should protect life and property until the organization was effected, provide a mode and method of organization, and superintend, by such means as should appear wise and proper, the process of organization.

In pursuance of this power, Congress, on the 2d of March, 1867, passed the original "reconstruction act," declaring that no legal civil government existed in certain States, (including the State of Georgia,) and conferring the whole government of the same upon the several commanders of the district therein provided for, but authorizing them to make use, in their discretion, of any civil organization they might find in existence. (Sections 1—3.)

This bill also provided that until the people of said States should be admitted to representation, any civil governments which may exist therein shall be deemed provisional only, and be subject to the paramount authority of the United States. (Section 6.)

It was also provided that this act should be inoperative whenever the people of said States, after the performance of certain conditions, should be admitted to representation in Congress. (Section 5.)

The preamble to said act recites its objects to be to preserve order until legal State governments should be legally established.

Very clearly under this act the whole effective power of preserving order and superintending the process of organization, is conferred upon the general commanding the several districts provided for.

The supplemental act of March 23, 1867, is still more emphatic upon this point. The commanding general is therein authorized to appoint registers, and generally clothed with the chief superintendence of the process of organization.

The additional supplemental act of July 19, 1867, is more emphatic still, declaring in express language that the said "governments," if continued, were to be subject in all respects to the military commanders.

The commanders are declared not to be bound in their construction of the law by the opinion of any civil officers of the United States.

It is also enacted that the several acts are to be construed liberally to the ends that the intents thereof may be fully and perfectly carried out, which intents, by the preamble to the original act, are declared to be the establishment of loyal republican State governments.

In pursuance of these acts, the military commanders have uniformly exercised, at their discretion, such powers of civil government and such powers of superintendence over the process of organization as in their judgment was best calculated to effect the object sought by Congress, to wit, the organization of loyal State governments in accordance with the Constitution and laws of the United States.

To this end they have removed officers, suspended laws, given authoritative interpretation to laws, and generally acted as supreme arbiters of every question which presented itself, not clearly provided for by act of Congress.

General Grant, in his report as Secretary of War, November, 1867, declares that the powers of these commanders are civil as well as military, and that in their civil capacity they are independent of even the General of the Army and Secretary of War, and commends them in the following terms:

"It is but fair to the district commanders, however, to state that while they have been thus independent in their civil duties, there has not been one of them who would not yield to a positively expressed wish in regard to any matter of civil administration from either of the officers placed over them by the Constitution or acts of Congress, so long as that wish was in the direction of a proper execution of the law, for the execution of which they are alone responsible." (McPherson's Manual, 1868, p. 314.)

It would appear, therefore, to be incontestable, that by the express language of the reconstruction acts, by the practice of the generals commanding the various districts, and by the opinions of the General of the Army and the Secretary of War, that the full superintendence of the process of reconstruction, and the authoritative interpretation of the law in all doubtful questions, is in the military commanders of the several "military districts," provided for by the act of March 2, 1867, and unless there be something in the peculiar status of Georgia, or in the acts of June 25, 1868, and December 22, 1869, modifying this power, under the circumstances the right of the Commanding General to "investigate" the eligibility of the claimants to seats is unquestionable.

The act of June 25, 1868, recognizing the "Constitution" as republican and fixing the terms in which the State should be admitted to representation, clearly contemplates (section 2) that the Legislatures shall be convened by the Governor elect, and not by the General Commanding: and this, too, is clearly the intent of the act of December 22, 1869, and in this particular the powers of the General Commanding are by both of these acts transferred to the Governor.

But in neither of these acts is there any special provision as to the mode and manner in which the Legislature shall organize.

In July, 1868, the several Houses were separately convened, the members qualified, and the organization effected under the direction of the Provisional Governor, with the concurrence and advice of General Meade, no reference at all being had in the organization to the eligibility of the members under the act of June 25, 1868.

When the organization was nominally complete, the two Houses

31

notified the fact to the Provisional Governor, who, on the same day notified the same to General Meade, with the suggestion that various persons had been permitted to participate who were disqualified.

To this General Meade replied, in substance, that in his judgment neither House was organized until all persons disqualified under the reconstruction acts were excluded—"that ordinarily each House would be the proper judge of the qualifications of its members, but inasmuch as it was his duty, so long as the government was provisional, to see that the laws were obeyed, he would not recognize the Legislature or any of its acts until satisfactory evidence was produced to him that all persons disqualified by the reconstruction laws were deprived of seats." (General Meade's Report, page 65.)

Upon this the several Houses proceeded to an investigation, and reported "that all the members of both Houses were eligible."

This report being communicated to General Meade, he announced that "he had no further opposition to make to their proceeding to the business for which they were called together." (General Meade's Report, pages 64 to 71.)

It will be noticed that General Meade did not at all think he had no power to interfere. His power was supreme, although he might, as he saw fit, use the civil organization or fail to use it, at his pleasure, and after he had used it he might overrule its action accordingly, as he was or was not, on the whole, satisfied that it was right.

In reference to this very matter he had, on July 6th, telegraphed to General Grant (Report, page 35,) and inquired, "If, in case the Legislature failed to purge itself, he had power to control the matter."

July 8, 1868, General Grant answers: "No person unable to hold office under the fourteenth amendment should be allowed to qualify. District commanders are the judges of the qualifications of civil officers until all the requirements of the different acts of Congress to complete reconstruction of the seceded States are fully complied with."

General Rawlins, Chief of Staff, also telegraphed a reply concluding thus:

"The reconstruction acts are to be construed liberally, to the end that all the intents thereof, to wit: the reëstablishment of civil government in the States lately in rebellion, may be fully and perfectly carried out, and it would seem that persons ineligible to hold office under their provisions should not be permitted to defeat them."

General Meade, in his dispatch of July 18, 1868, to General Grant, informing him what he had determined to do, to not regard the action of the two Houses as final, says:

"My judgment, therefore, is to acquiesce in the decision of the Senate (and House) and leave to Congress such action as may hereafter be deemed proper, in case the Senate (and House) has failed to comply with the law;" and concludes his dispatch thus:

"What I desire to know is, whether in your judgment my duty requires me to overrule the deliberate act of the Senate, and judge for myself on the qualifications of the members.

" I have no doubt of my power in the premises, but do not feel that I am called on to do more than I have done." (General Meade's Report, page 38.)

It is very apparent, therefore, that while General Meade was disposed under the circumstances to acquiesce in the decision of the two Houses, he had no doubt of his power to interfere: that in fact he did not feel called on to overrule the action of the body to which he had referred it, but submitted the whole to the judgment of Congress.

The "judgment of Congress" is announced by the act of December 22, 1869.

This act has for its whole purpose the intent to repair the mistake made by Major General Meade, in permitting the very body to be purged to be made up in the first instance of those who were to be excluded by the purging process.

It is generally contended that the Congress of the United States, as a means of curing the mistake of Major General Meade, in taking as conclusive of eligibility the deliberate legislative judgment of the several Houses as political bodies, has been guilty of the absurdity of making the judgment of the very men who are charged to be ineligible, the sole criterion of eligibility.

Dissatisfied with the judgment of the body itself, and holding that not conclusive, Congress has made each member the judge of his own eligibility. What the whole body deliberately failed to do is left to be done, and that without appeal, by the very individual members whom it is charged were improperly admitted. So preposterous a conclusion ought to have very clear and positive language in the law to support it, and ought only to be arrived at when the words of the law inevitably compel such a construction.

The act of December 22 has not in it a single word limiting the power of the general commanding, save that it, as did also the act of June 25, 1868, contemplates that the Legislature shall be convened by the order of the Governor.

It would be a gross misconception of this law to construe it by itself. It must be read and understood in connection with the other acts upon the same subject.

Its title announces that it is an act to "promote the reconstruction of Georgia."

It assumes that the reconstruction of the State is still incomplete ; that the government existing in the State is still provisional, and "subject," in the words of the act of July 19, 1867, "in all respects, to the military commander of the district," and "to the paramount authority of Congress," and is to be construed as additional and supplemental to the reconstruction acts, and not as an independent act. It leaves, therefore, the authority of the Military Commander precisely where the other acts placed it, except as that authority is modified by the act itself.

The oath prescribed is merely cumulative, an additional safeguard in aid of the powers of the General Commanding.

It is a fundamental idea of the whole reconstruction policy, that no person shall hold office in the late rebel States who has held office and then afterward engaged in rebellion, unless he be relieved from disabilities by a two-thirds vote of Congress.

And it is trifling with that whole policy to permit, if there be

any possible means to prevent it, the very first Legislature, before
reconstruction is complete, and while the military jurisdiction is
still paramount, to be organized in defiance of that policy, with
the vain hope that after the organization is complete, the body,
which so signally failed before, will itself purge itself of its ineligible members.

So long as the State is denied representation by Congress, the
power of the General Commanding is complete. He may, as did
General Meade, in his discretion, refer the question to the Legislature, but the success of that experiment, and the subsequent action of Congress, has not been such as to justify the repetition of the
farce, much less to infer that such was the intent of Congress.

The act, so far from making the oath of the member conclusive,
or contemplating that the question shall be left to the bodies after
they are organized, when fairly considered, has directly the oppo-
site meaning.

It provides (section 1) that the Legislature shall proceed to organize "under the laws of the United States."

It provides further (section 4) that the persons so declared elected
"and entitled to seats, and who shall take the oaths provided,
shall." &c.

It provides (section 3) that it shall be illegal to prevent any person elected as aforesaid, who has taken one of the oaths prescribed,
and otherwise complied with this act, from participating, &c.

It provides (section 6) that it shall be illegal and revolutionary
to exclude any one elected as aforesaid, and otherwise qualified,
from participation because of his race or color.

By section 4 it is not enough, by the very terms of the act, that
he shall have been elected and taken the oaths, he must be entitled
to a seat.

It is not enough, by section 5, that he shall have taken the oath,
he must have otherwise complied with the provisions of the law.

It is not enough, by section 5, that he is elected, to make it illegal to exclude him from his race or color. He must be otherwise
qualified.

If the taking of the oath is to be conclusive, why should the Congress also say "and be entitled to a seat," "have otherwise complied," and "he be otherwise qualified?"

It is a fair mode of consideration to assume that each word
and phrase of an act has a meaning, and there can be no conceivable reason why the act should say "elected," "take the
oaths," "be entitled to a seat," "and be otherwise qualified,"
unless it was meant that there might be cases where one has been
elected and taken the oath and yet not be entitled to a seat: especially is this construction proper if it be considered that the
whole necessity for the act grows out of the fact that in July,
1868, not only many individual members were sworn in who were
ineligible, but a majority of the two houses determined, after (as
it was said) full investigation, that there were no ineligible members in either house.

That the oath of the members is conclusive is simply absurd.
It is the ordinary course of legislative bodies to inquire into the
eligibility of members after they have taken the oath. The Georgia constitution requires that each member shall swear that he

E

has not obtained his election illegally. Is that oath conclusive? May not the house investigate the facts, and if they be found otherwise, may it not declare him illegally elected? The only question there can be, under the law, is, whether the power to determine the question is not in the body itself.

Ordinarily, as General Meade and General Rawlins say, and as the practice is, this is a power in the body itself, and, without question, the Commanding General might, as did General Meade, in his discretion, refer it to them. But so long as the reconstruction laws are not fully complied with, it is the right of the General Commanding to see to it that the laws are complied with, and under the experience of July, 1868, and the action of Congress, it would seem that in such a question as this, so vital to the organization of the Legislature, so distasteful as this rule of ineligibility has proven to the reactionary party, that its final decision ought to be neither with the member himself nor with the body which has in a former trial proven so unwilling to enforce the rule upon its members.

To permit one who is ineligible to take part in the oaganization of the body which is to decide his case, may not be a very great evil, but when the charge of ineligibility includes a member, it is obvious that if they be permitted to become members in fact, it will be almost impossible to unseat them.

Ordinarily there is no other method, because there is no superior power; but in the status of affairs as they exist now in Georgia, there is such a power, and an occasion plainly calling for its interference.

What is to be gained in the promotion of reconstruction by repeating the proceedings of July, 1868? With the act of Congress staring them in the face, that no person was eligible to office who had held office before the rebellion, and thereafter engaged in rebellion, these very men deliberately took the oath of office, and a majority of each house declared them all eligible. Congress has reversed the proceedings, declared the Houses not properly organized, provided for a reorganization, and it is contended that of necessity the same process of individual judgment and organized indorsement shall be repeated, and this, too, with a paramount authority looking on and seeing with its own eyes a repetition of the sham of July, 1868, actually progressing.

So much upon the first branch of the question, the power of the general commanding to "investigate" the question of ineligibility, and to prevent the failure of the whole Congressional scheme by the recklessness of those who are ready to move heaven and earth to work its discomfiture.

But there is a second question. There are from fifteen to eighteen of those declared elected by General Meade who have neglected, refused, and are doubtless unable to take the oath, and who are by express language of the law declared to be ineligible. There are from ten to fifteen more who *may* be found ineligible by the commission now sitting. The question arises, Shall the House proceed to organize with only such of its legal members as are here and have taken the oath, or shall those who received the next highest vote at the election be notified to appear, and if they are eligible be permitted to take the oath and participate in the organization?

There can be no question that it is the law of Georgia that the votes cast at an election for one who is ineligible to the position are not to be counted, and it is the duty of the Governor who issues the commission, if he be satisfied that the highest man is ineligible, to give the commission to the next highest who is eligible.

He is declared by the code to be the person legally elected, and he is entitled to the certificate of election.

The proclamation of General Meade only purports to be based upon the returns, and such was in truth the basis of the order. It is not at all based on the eligibility of the persons named, but upon the simple fact that the returns show the persons named to have received the highest vote.

Had the question of eligibility been presented to General Meade before that proclamation was made—had the board upon whose report it is founded taken the eligibility of the persons named into consideration, perhaps the list would have been very different, since, by the law of Georgia, they would have been compelled to declare elected in every case where the highest was ineligible the person who was next highest if he was eligible. Such was not, however, the course then pursued, though it was a course perfectly consonant with the law of the State.

That the general commanding may do now what might have been done then is unquestionable, unless there be something in the act of December 22, 1869, forbidding this and prescribing a different course. What is the fact?

The bill directs the Governor to convene by proclamation those declared elected by General Meade's order of June 25, 1868. And it further provides that when the members "so elected," not so "declared elected," shall convene, each "member" and each and every person "claiming to be elected" shall take the oath, &c., and every person "claiming to be so elected who shall refuse, decline, neglect, or be unable to take the oath, shall not be admitted to a seat or to participate in the proceedings," but shall be "deemed ineligible to such seats."

Section 3 provides that if any person "claiming" to be elected as aforesaid—that is, to a seat in the Senate or House—shall take the oath falsely, &c.

The whole language of the bill is evidently used in reference to the code of Georgia, which declares that the second highest is the person elected if the "highest" is ineligible, and clearly contemplates that no person ineligible, though he may claim to be "elected," is not in fact "so elected." It will be noticed that the words so often used in the act are not "so declared elected," but "so elected," or "claiming to be so elected." The word "so" does not refer to the proclamation, but "so elected," and claiming to be so elected, refers to the Senate or House of Representatives respectively, and the word "so" is used to save the frequent repetition of those words.

The persons elected to the Senate and House of Representatives of Georgia are, by the law of Georgia, those who got the highest vote if they are eligible, and those who got the next highest vote in cases where the highest are ineligible.

These classes, and these only, are the persons who fill the description of section 3, to wit: "The persons elected as aforesaid—that is, elected to the Senate and House respectively—who shall take the oath and shall proceed in said Senate and House, to which they have been elected, to reorganize the same."

Under the laws of Georgia, nobody who is ineligible is elected. If an ineligible person gets the highest vote, he is not elected; but the next highest is.

And the peculiar language of the act of December 22, 1869, is a clear indication that it was drawn with special reference to the Georgia law, which the unseating of the negroes and the admission of the next highest as the persons elected, had brought prominently before the eyes of Congress.

That the general commanding has, by virtue of his assignment to the command to the "district" of Georgia, full powers in the premises is, as has been shown, unquestionable; and that the act of December 22, 1869, does not, in this respect, qualify those powers, is equally clear; and there would appear to be, therefore, no good reason why the law of Georgia should not, in the discretion of the general commanding, be applied to the case.

It will close up the whole matter; it will put the new government in the hands of its friends; it will secure the fifteenth amendment; it will enable the friends of the new constitution to carry its provisions into effect in good faith, and close up rapidly and healthfully the sore which since 1865 has been irritating the body politic.

To secure such ends a liberal interpretation of the reconstruction acts is specifically required, and would be in accordance with the whole policy of Congress, to wit, to set the new government afloat under the guidance of the friends of reconstruction, and not under the control of those who have in every conceivable way tried to thwart and obstruct its success. Many of its most important provisions are in the eyes of these enemies to it odious in the extreme, and it is saying but little to suggest that they will not give it a fair and liberal trial. If, unfortunately, these men succeed, their past course indicates that they will be no true friends to its fundamental ideas, and a wise public policy would seem to indicate that while the hand of authority is still raised the door for revolution should be closed.

Section 121 of the code of Georgia, to which reference has been made as fixing the effect of ineligibility, is in these words: "If, at any popular election to fill any office, the person elected is ineligible under one of the foregoing rules, the person having the next highest number of votes, who is eligible when a plurality elects, shall be declared elected and be qualified and commissioned to such office."

It will be noticed that this act applies to every popular election to fill any office, whenever a plurality elects.

At the date of the code, December 19, 1860, the Governor and judges of the superior courts were required to be elected by a majority vote; all other officers were simply to be elected. So too is the constitution of 1865. The constitution of 1868, which addcts the

37

code as the system of law, provides that the person having the majority of the whole number of votes cast, shall be declared duly elected Governor. The only other officers of the State elective by the people are the members of the general assembly, county officers, and justices of the peace; these, the constitution says, shall be elected by the qualified voters, &c. The fact that of the several elections provided for, to wit: Governor, members of the Legislature, county officers, and justices of the peace, only one is required to have the majority of all the votes cast, is conclusive that it was the intent that at all elections except for Governor, a plurality elects.

Such has always been the understanding of the law in this State, and such was the rule adopted by General Meade in issuing the proclamation of June 25, 1868, as will abundantly appear by an examination of the returns. The law of Georgia has always required a majority in the case of the election of the "Governor," and, for awhile, of judges of the superior court, but never for any other officer. Such at least has always been the practice. It is based not only on the general rules of the common law, but on the rule that, as the constitution required specially a "majority" in the cases of Governor, it left other elections to be decided by a plurality vote. It follows, therefore, that, under the law of Georgia, if the member of the Legislature having the highest vote is ineligible, the person having the next highest, who is eligible, is to be declared elected and to be qualified and commissioned to such office.

Ordinarily, as I have said, the duty of investigating the eligibility of members of the Legislature is with that body, and, without question, if a person nominally elected is found ineligible, that body would declare the next highest elected and give him the seat.

Such was the action of the Legislature in July, 1868, in the case of "Bradley," senator.

Bradley was found ineligible, by reason of having been convicted of "felony," and his seat was given to Lester, the next highest at the election.

This was done before the colored members were expelled, and on this point the action of the senate in that case was universally acquiesced in.

Indeed, there never has been in the State any doubts of the application of this law to the Legislature, until the present crisis has given it birth.

If the commanding general has the power, as most unquestionably he has, to "investigate" the eligibility of a member and "decide" upon it, and exclude him, it would seem to follow (as by the ordinance he is required to issue certificates of election) that the right of the next highest immediately to be declared elected by him, must be the inevitable consequence.

The power to investigate and decide involves the power to cause the decision to be carried into its full effect; the exclusion of the ineligible member is but a part of the effect; the full decision is not only that the ineligible person is not elected, but that the eligible one is.

APPENDIX C.

The question whether a person who at the election held on the 20th, 21st, 22d, and 23d of April, 1868, received within his district the second highest number of votes for a seat in the Legislature of Georgia, he being eligible thereto, is entitled to the seat in case the person who received the highest number of votes is ineligible under the fourteenth amendment to the Constitution of the United States, is presented in a double aspect.

First, it is claimed that by the express provisions of the law of Georgia he is so entitled.

Secondly, it is claimed that by the general or common law on the subject, he is so entitled.

On the first point, certain classes of persons are declared by the law of Georgia to be ineligible to office, and it is provided that " If at any popular election to fill any office, the person elected is ineligible under the foregoing rules, the person receiving the next highest number of votes, who is eligible, whenever a plurality elects, shall be declared elected and be qualified and commissioned to such office." (Irwin's Code, page 33 and 34.)

The only one of the foregoing rules referred to which can apply in this case is that which declares that "all persons from any cause *constitutionally* disqualified," are ineligible.

The question thus resolves itself into this : Were persons who had held any one of the offices mentioned in the fourteenth amendment to the Constitution of the United States, and thereafter entered into the rebellion, *constitutionally* disqualified for office at the time the election of April, 1868, was held?

If at that time any State constitution was in existence in Georgia, it must have been the constitution of 1798.

The constitution certainly contained no such provisions as those of the fourteenth amendment. If the rebellion and attempted secession operated to destroy the State government, and with it the State constitution—and this seems to be the position taken by Congress in providing for the reconstruction of the rebel States—then there existed at that time no State constitution by the provisions of which any person, for any cause, could have been disqualified.

Were such persons disqualified by the Constitution of the *United States?*

The election was held on the 20th, 21st, 22d, and 23d days of April, 1868. The fourteenth amendment was not declared to be a part of the Constitution until the 21st day of July, 1868.

It is true that by the sixth section of the act of March 2, 1867, the provisions of the amendment were applied to the States lately in rebellion, and it was declared that "no person shall be eligible

to any office under any such provisional government, who would
be disqualified from holding office under the third article of said
constitutional amendment;" but this was a statutory provision,
not a constitutional one; and it created a statutory disqualification, not a constitutional one.

Thus it seems plain that there was then no *constitutional* disqualification of any kind, on account of participation in the rebellion, and that, therefore, the above mentioned provisions of the
statute of Georgia have no application to the case.

The second point remains to be considered.

In England, the country from which we mainly derive our parliamentary law, a plurality elects, and votes are given orally.
There, it is absolutely established by a long course of decisions
that if notice be given of the disqualification of a candidate, every
vote given for him afterward is thrown away, and will be considered as not given at all—as void—as not to be counted as
against the person who receives the next highest vote. The principle upon which this is done is a plain one. It is this, viz: The
electors at any election are not called upon by the law to signify
whom they would choose to hold a given office without restriction.
They are called upon to signify *which one of those who are eligible*
they would choose; and he who votes for an ineligible person fails
to do that which the law calls upon him to do, and in contempla-
tion of law does not vote at all.

Much confusion on this subject has arisen in the popular mind
from the celebrated case of Wilkes and Luttrell; but I believe
that it will be found that through that protracted struggle the
principle that the candidate having the next highest number of
votes is entitled to the office, in case the candidate receiving the
highest number is ineligible, *was never denied.* The point in issue
was the question of Wilkes' eligibility; he had been expelled from
the House of Commons, and had been declared ineligible to a
reëlection by a vote of that body; and it was contended that while
that House could expel him it could not *disfranchise* him, that it
could not make him ineligible to a reëlection, that no Englishman
could be disfranchised except by act of Parliament, the concur-
rent action of King, Lords, and Commons; and this point was
finally yielded by the Government and its supporters.

Cushing, (Law and Practice of Legislative Assemblies, pp.
66-67,) after stating the law of England, proceeds to lay down the
law in this country, as follows, viz:

"178. In this country, it is equally true, that the election of a
disqualified person is absolutely void; and, in those States where a
plurality elects, and where the votes are given orally, as in England, votes given for a candidate after notice of his disqualification are thrown away, and the candidate having the next highest
number of votes is elected.

"179. In reference to elections by ballot, in which secrecy is the
distinguishing feature; and, in which, consequently, neither the
returning officers, nor the electors themselves, are supposed to
know for whom the votes are given, until the result is declared; it
seems not unreasonable to consider the votes for ineligible candidates to be thrown away, in all cases, and the opposing candidate
elected, where the electors know or must be presumed to know the

disability; and, in all cases where there is no such actual or presumed knowledge, to hold the whole proceeding merely void.

"180. In reference to elections, in which an absolute majority is requisite to a choice, and in which, consequently, the whole number of votes received is first to be ascertained, votes given for ineligible persons must of course be excluded from the enumeration; for the reason that, as the whole balloting would be void, and all the votes excluded if they were all for such candidates, it would be preposterous to enumerate such votes, where they constituted only a part of the votes given in. If, in consequence of such exclusion, the result of the election would be different from what it would otherwise be, the whole proceeding must perhaps be held void or valid, according as the electors have actual or presumed knowledge of the ineligibility of the persons for whom the excluded votes are given."

It will be observed that a distinction is here made between votes given orally and those given by ballot—a distinction justly founded on the necessity of the case. Voters who vote orally must be notified of the disqualification of their candidate. Those who vote by ballot, i e. secretly, are not entitled to actual notice. The law laid down by Cushing has recently received the sanction of the House of Representatives of the United States. Mr. John D. Young was elected a member of the House, in the Fortieth Congress, from the Ninth Congressional District of Kentucky, by a majority of votes, but he was found and declared to be ineligible by reason of his inability to take the prescribed oaths of office, and his competitor at the election, Mr.—— McKee, although he received only a minority of the votes, was admitted to a seat in his stead.

It seems to me that this precedent, coupled with the authority of Cushing, should be considered as settling the law as far as elections held under Acts of Congress in the States lately in rebellion are concerned.

But it has been said that the disability must have existed at the time of the election—that the candidate must have been absolutely and clearly ineligible at that time, and that the doctrine that the next highest candidate is entitled does not apply where the disability might be removed by act of Congress. In regard to this latter position, one thing seems clear, viz: that it is absolutely, and diametrically opposed to the practice and decisions in England. Were it to prevail there no votes could be excluded from the count, and "no next highest" candidate could be entitled to an office, for there is, and can be, under the theory of the English Constitution, no disqualification which may not be removed by an act of Parliament.

Might it not as well be contended that votes for a notorious felon just convicted of his crime should be counted because by a bare possibility an appeal from the judgment of the court before which he was convicted might be taken, or a writ of error brought, and thereupon that judgment reversed? That the disability must have existed *at the time* is undoubtedly true: no subsequently occurring disability can justify the rejection of a vote; and that the disqualification must have been clear and absolute is equally true.

It has been said, and is undoubtedly true, that the failure of the

41

person who received the highest number of votes to qualify after the election, as by refusing or neglecting to take a required official oath, cannot justify the rejection of the votes cast for him: but it may be observed that leaving out of view the question of notice to the voter, the fact of such failure to qualify may become a part of the evidence of disqualification.

To apply these principles to the case in question: By the sixth section of the act of Congress of March 2d, 1867, already cited, it is provided that "no person shall be eligible to any office under such provisional governments who would be disqualified from holding office under the provisions of the third article of said constitutional amendment," (referring to the fourteenth amendment) thus putting that article in force in the rebel States in advance of its adoption as a part of the Constitution of the United States. A disqualification for holding office was thus created by a statute of which every person had actual or presumed notice. Subsequent to the passage of that statute, an election was held and certain persons received the highest number of votes, several of whom at the recent reorganization of the Legislature refused, neglected, or were unable to take the oath which had been provided as a *test of their eligibility*, and in addition thereto, filed with the Provisional Governor of the State *applications to Congress for a removal of their disabilities*, thus *admitting* their ineligibility to office under the fourteenth amendment. It must be remembered that although the fourteenth amendment was not adopted until after the election at which these persons were elected, its provisions were in force in the States lately in rebellion by virtue of the statute, and that if these persons are ineligible now under the amendment, they were ineligible at the time of the election under the statute. It is no new disability which has been imposed.

I think that the fact of the ineligibility is therefore fully proven.

Must the electors be charged with notice of the ineligibility of these persons?

They must, of course, be charged with knowledge of the law, and when it is remembered that the ineligibility in question grew out of the then and still recent events of a great civil war, in which the greatest interest was felt by every person living within the territory of the nation; grew out of *public* events of the most transcendent importance, to which the attention of every person was irresistably attracted; that the terms of reconstruction had been made the subject of excited and angry controversy, that the fact of the holding of office prior to the rebellion must have been a matter of public notoriety, and the participation or non-participation of any person in the rebellion must have been well known in the community in which he lived, I think that it is hardly possible to relieve the voters from the presumption of knowledge of disqualification. Therefore, under the rule laid down by Cushing, and under the decision of the House of Representatives, I think that those who received the next highest votes to these persons are entitled to seats.

F

APPENDIX D.

Mr. Caldwell, in his printed paper, divides the latter portion of it under the head of "Governor Bullock's personal attack."

It is with great reluctance that I have obtained my own consent to take any notice whatever in connection with a subject of such grave importance as that which the honorable Judiciary Committee now have under consideration, of anything of a personal character. But, as Mr. Caldwell has seen fit to attribute my transmission of a letter addressed to me by the Hon. Foster Blodgett, setting forth information that was conveyed to him by Mr. J. Mason Rice, as a personal attack upon him, I will say that I believe the statement made by Mr. Rice to Mr. Blodgett, and to Hon. C. H. Prince, as alleged in that letter, is true.

I also invite your attention to the copy of a letter (marked E) addressed to me by the Hon. A. L. Harris, of Atlanta, dated February 22, 1870, which refutes the assertion made by Mr. Caldwell, that "Mr. A. L. Harris, the Governor's clerk *pro tem.*, and railroad supervisor, said to me that I should have any place I wanted in his department if I would yield my opposition to the Governor."

E.

ATLANTA, GA., *February 22,* 1870.

To His Excellency R. B. Bullock, Governor:

SIR: In a pamphlet purporting to be the "Argument of Hon. J. H. Caldwell and Hon. J. E. Bryant before the Judiciary Committee of the United States Senate," occur these words from Mr. Caldwell:

"Mr. A. L. Harris, the Governor's clerk *pro tem.*, and Railroad Supervisor, said to me that I should have any place I wanted in his department if I would yield my opposition to the Governor."

The above statement is entirely incorrect. I remember one afternoon, at the National Hotel, having seen Rev. J. H. Caldwell and Mr. J. Mason Rice in conversation, and just after Mr. Rice left Mr. Caldwell I passed that way, when Mr. Caldwell asked me if, provided he supported Governor Bullock and the Republican party, he and his family would be taken care of on the State Road; or, in other words, would they get good paying positions?

I told him to see the Superintendent, as he alone had the power of making appointments. He intimated that he would like the Senatorship for the long term, while he desired his two brothers and their sons, and his own son, to have lucrative positions on the road.

I never said to Mr. Caldwell that he "should have any place he
wanted in my department," neither did I say anything of that
tenor, or that could be construed into anything of the kind.
Very respectfully,

A. L. HARRIS.

I am also informed that one or two of the brothers and a son of
Mr. Caldwell are or were employed on the State railroad.

Each one of the persons whose names are printed on Mr. Cald-
well's pamphlet as a "delegation"—namely, J. E. Bryant, J. H.
Caldwell. C. K. Osgood, A. J. Williams, N. L. Angier, and John
Bowles—are either disappointed aspirants for position under the
late legislative organization, warm personal friends of Mr. Joshua
Hill, or persons who fear an investigation by the Legislature.

Mr. Bryant, as is well known, is the defeated Democratic candidate for Speaker. Mr. Caldwell is disappointed in Senatorial
aspirations. Mr. C. K. Osgood and Mr. A. J. Williams are very
clever gentlemen, who believe that Mr. Joshua Hill is the greatest
statesman that the world ever produced. Mr. John Bowles is the
son-in-law of Mr. Hill. He was collector of internal revenue at
Augusta under appointment from ex-President Johnson, but was
removed by President Grant, and a worthy colored man appointed
in his place.

The party whose name appears in this list as "N. L. Angier,
State Treasurer," will necessarily receive a much more extended
notice.

He presents, with the others, a paper, entitled "Governor Bullock's Financial Operations," every word of which has been
iterated and reiterated through the Democratic newspapers of
Georgia in various ways and shapes since Mr. Angier allied himself with the revolutionizing Democrats of the Legislature.

Every charge in it has been publicly refuted, and need not here
receive attention, except the reissue of a statement formerly made
by him which I have not heretofore noticed, namely: "On the
21st day of November, 1868, the cashier of the Georgia National
Bank presented the Governor's draft on the Fourth National
Bank of New York for $25,000, and voluntarily stated that it was
to cover Governor Bullock's individual indebtedness to this
bank."

In answer to this I invite your attention to the copy of a letter
from the cashier of the Georgia National Bank, that came to me
about the time of the publication of this matter last summer, and
which has not previously been used by myself. This letter is
appended below:

GEORGIA NATIONAL BANK,
ATLANTA, GA., August 29, 1869.

To His Excellency, Governor Bullock:

DEAR SIR: Referring to Treasurer Angier's letter to the people of Georgia, of August 27th, published in this morning's New
Era, I find the following statement:

"In contrast to this pitiful amount received by the Treasurer,
but since paid into the Treasury, that officer will present to the

public a few instances of the illegal uses of the State funds by the Executive for his own benefit. On the 21st November, 1868, when the State had sufficient funds on hand to meet all reasonable expenses, (having on the day previous drawn twenty-five thousand dollars) ($25,000,) the Cashier of the Georgia National Bank presented the Governor's draft on the Temporary Loans for *twenty-five thousand dollars* ($25,000) *more*, and voluntarily stated that Governor Bullock was indebted to their Bank *seventeen thousand dollars* ($17,000,) and this twenty-five thousand dollars *was to cover up and make good to the Bank the Governor's individual indebtedness*, although said deposit was placed to the credit of the State. The State was thus forced to pay, as per statement of Cashier, nearly *eleven per cent.* on this twenty-five thousand dollars, drawn *solely* as an offset, for the time being, against the individual deficit of the Governor."

In regard to the State having on hand sufficient funds to meet all reasonable expenses, &c., I have to say, that the Treasury balance, as appears by the books of the Bank, on the 21st November, 1868, after the draft of $25,000 had been deposited to his credit, was $35,308 95, and that between that time and the 30th of the same month, we paid his checks to the amount of $24,286 50. In addition to that amount we paid his checks during the first week of December to the amount of $19,840 15. From this you will see that the $25,000 was positively necessary to meet the requirements of the Treasury, and was drawn from the Bank in less than ten days, and had not the draft been deposited, his account would have been largely overdrawn.

The statement contained in the paragraph quoted above that when "the Cashier of the Georgia National Bank presented the Governor's draft on the temporary loans for $25,000 more, voluntarily stated that Governor Bullock was indebted to their bank $17,000, and this $25,000 was to cover up and make good to the Bank the Governor's individual indebtedness," I pronounce as positively untrue.

I deem it but simple justice to you, as well as to myself, that I make this statement.

Very respectfully, your obedient servant,

E. L. JONES.

The second statement is as follows: "He has paid out of the State treasury nearly two thousand dollars to light Kimball's Opera-house, when the building had not been used for State purposes over six times at night; none of the State offices being kept open at nights." This, of course, amounts to a direct charge that, with my knowledge and consent, the State treasury was charged with a large sum of money to pay for light which was not used for the benefit of the State. To show that this statement was made by Mr. Angier, with a knowledge of its falsity and with a deliberate purpose to misrepresent facts which were known to him, I ask attention to the following papers:

ATLANTA, GA., *September* 8, 1869.

Charles C. Rodes, Esq., Superintendent Atlanta Gas Light Company,
Atlanta, Ga.

DEAR SIR: Please inform me as to how the gas pipes and meters
are located in Kimball's Opera House, used as the State Capitol,
and by whom the gas used in the different stores and rooms in the
building is paid for.

Very respectfully, yours,

J. A. BURNS,

Keeper, &c.

ATLANTA GASLIGHT COMPANY'S OFFICE, *Sept.* 10, 1869.

J. A. Burns, Esq., Keeper of Capitol, &c.:

SIR: Yours of 8th asking how the gas pipes are arranged and
meters located, and by whom the gas is paid for in the Kimball
Opera House, used as the State Capitol, is at hand, and, in answer,
have to say that the gas used in the cafe, billiard rooms, and res-
taurant passes through a distinct meter set expressly for that purpose, and is paid for by Mr. Thompson. The gas used on the fifth
floor or dormitories has also a separate meter, and is paid for by
Mr. H. I. Kimball. The gas for store No. 3 has a separate meter,
and is paid for by Mr. Walker. The telegraph office has a meter,
gas paid for by the telegraph company. The gas used in stores
Nos. 5 and 6 passes through one meter for both, and was paid for
by Mr. Cook when he occupied them, since then what has been
used has been paid for by Mr. Kimball. The State has two large
meters, one of which supplies the House of Representatives,
Senate Chamber, Caucus Rooms, and corridors leading thereto on
the second floor, and the offices of Controller General, Secretary
of State, Surveyor, and corridors on the first floor. The other
supplies the Library, Court Room and Treasurer's Office on first
floor, and all other portions of the building used by the State.

The gas consumed during the session of the Legislature last
winter, and what has been used since in the different offices and
corridors, has been paid for by the State, which bills have been
and are yet rendered quarterly. The other consumers settle
monthly. There are seven meters in the building, and no gas
passes through either of the State meters but what is used for
State purposes.

Respectfully, yours,

CHARLES C. RODES,

Superintendent Atlanta Gaslight Company.

ATLANTA, GEORGIA, *September* 10, 1869.

Mr. J. A. Burns, Keeper, &c.

DEAR SIR: We have read the foregoing letter to you, from Mr.
Rodes. We put up the gas pipes, chandeliers, &c., used in light-
ing Kimball's Opera House, used as the State Capitol; and there-

fore, of our own knowledge, can say that statements of Mr. Rodes as to the location of the meters and rooms supplied through them are correct.

Respectfully yours, &c.,
HUNNICUTT & ZELLINGRUTH,
Plumbers and Gas Fitters.

ATLANTA, GA., *October* 8, 1869.
His EXCELLENCY RUFUS B. BULLOCK,
Governor of Georgia, Atlanta, Ga.:

SIR: I have the honor to transmit herewith a communication from Charles C. Rodes, Superintendent of the Atlantic Gas Works, in relation to the location of the gas-pipes and meters in the "Opera House," used as the State Capitol. In conversation with Mr. Rodes, he said that he had explained to Hon. N. L. Angier, Treasurer, the manner in which gas was supplied to the different rooms in the "Opera House," and by whom it was paid for, giving him, in substance, all the information contained in his (Rodes) letter to me herewith transmitted. Mr. Rodes made this explanation to Hon. N. L. Angier sometime last spring, and therefore the Treasurer was in possession of these facts when he wrote his address "To the People of Georgia," under date of August 27, 1869, and published in the Atlanta *New Era.*

I am, sir, very respectfully, your obedient servant,
J. A. BURNS,
Keeper Public Property, &c.

One moving motive for the action of Angier, in his efforts to prevent a full recognition of the reorganization of the Legislature, is the great probability that he will not be retained as Treasurer.

At the next session of the Superior Court, the suit of the State against Angier and his bondsmen will be called for trial, and he and his bondsmen will be called upon to pay over $20,000 pains, fines, and penalties, for his violation of law in using the State's money and allowing others to use the same for his private benefit.

Much more could be said not to the credit of Messrs. Caldwell, Bryant, Angier, and Bowles, but I forbear.